Artists Through the Ages

Johannes Vermeer

Alix Wood

WINDMILL BOOKS™

New York

Published in 2013 by Windmill Books, An Imprint of Rosen Publishing
29 East 21st Street, New York, NY 10010

Editor for Alix Wood Books: Eloise Macgregor
US Editor: Sara Antill
Designer: Alix Wood

Photo Credits: Cover, 1, 11; © Artothek; 7 © Rijksmuseum; 8-9 © Blauel/
Gnamm - Artothek; 13 © Peter Willi - Artothek; 15 © Städel Museum -
Artothek; 16 © author; 17 © Artothek; 18 © Rijksmuseum; 20 © nga; 21 ©
Artothek; 23 © Photobusiness - Artothek; 24-25 © Artothek; 26 © ngs; 28 top
© Holly Hayes; 29 bottom © rangizzz - Fotolia 3, 4, 9 inset, 14, 19, 27, 28
bottom, 29 top © Shutterstock

Library of Congress Cataloging-in-Publication Data

Wood, Alix.
 Johannes Vermeer / by Alix Wood.
    p. cm. — (Artists through the ages)
 Includes index.
 ISBN 978-1-61533-623-4 (library binding) — ISBN 978-1-61533-633-3 (pbk.)
 — ISBN 978-1-61533-634-0 (6-pack)
 1. Vermeer, Johannes, 1632–1675—Juvenile literature. 2. Painters—
Netherlands—Biography—Juvenile literature. I. Title.
 ND653.V5W66 2013
 759.9492—dc23
 [B]

                    2012025843

Manufactured in the United States of America

CPSIA Compliance Information: Batch #BW13WM: For Further Information contact Windmill Books, New York, New York at 1-866-478-0556

Contents

Who Was Vermeer?

Johannes (or Jan) Vermeer is a rather mysterious artist. We don't know a lot about his life. Most people think the picture on the cover of this book is Vermeer, but even that isn't certain. Vermeer was born in the Netherlands in the city of Delft, and baptized in 1632. His father, Reijnier Janszoon, was an art dealer. Young Johannes became interested in art. When his father died in 1652, Vermeer took his place as an art dealer.

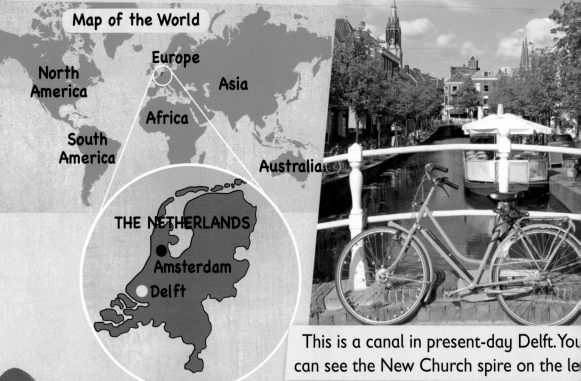

Map of the World

Europe

North America

Asia

Africa

South America

Australia

THE NETHERLANDS

Amsterdam

Delft

This is a canal in present-day Delft. You can see the New Church spire on the le

A map of Delft in 1652, by Willem Blaeu

1: The Flying Fox
2: The New Church
3: The Great Market
4: The Old Church

Vermeer is thought to have been born in an inn his father rented at the time called The Flying Fox. His father later bought another inn called Mechelen on the Great Market. While other artists of his time left the town to go to the cities of Amsterdam or Rotterdam, Vermeer lived and died in the little town of Delft.

Vermeer's Life

Growing up in a lively inn with an art dealer father, Vermeer would have had a lot of contact with artists and art dealers of the day. At the age of 21 he became a member of the St. Luke's Guild. This meant he could become a master art dealer like his father. The same year Vermeer married a **Catholic** girl named Catherine Bolnes. Catherine's mother, Maria Thins, at first refused to let them marry, perhaps because Vermeer was a **Protestant**. She eventually tolerated the marriage. Johannes and Catherine went on to have 14 children!

Sad Times

Children born in Vermeer's time often didn't survive for long. Of the 14 children Vermeer and his wife had, four died young. Church records show that in 1660 they buried a child at the Old Church. They were living at the time at Catherine's mother's house in Delft. In 1667 another child is buried at the New Church. In 1669 and 1673 there are further burials at Old Church.

Little Street, by Vermeer. What do you think the two children are playing?

View of Delft

Delft was a busy town in the seventeenth century. It had a skyline of church towers and monastery spires, and was surrounded by walls, gates, rivers, and watchtowers to keep the people safe from invaders. The river, the Old Delft, carried the traffic of ships and boats. The river water was very clean and perfect for brewing beer. Delft was considered the cleanest of all Dutch cities, and the Dutch were considered the cleanest of all Europe.

View of Delft, painted around 1659

Delft Blue

Delft was a center for **porcelain**. Delft blue tiles are famous throughout the world.

Is This Vermeer?

The smiling young man on the left of the painting opposite is believed to be a self-portrait of Vermeer. Many experts think Vermeer painted himself separately and then put it rather awkwardly into the picture. In many similar paintings of the time, an artist would paint himself staring out at the viewer, usually on the edge of a crowd and often wearing a hat and fancy costume. The artist would usually have a sly smile, be raising a glass, and holding a lute. The painting of this young man fits that perfectly, and Vermeer would have been about 24 when he painted this.

Mirror Image?

Some people think Vermeer painted this image of himself in a mirror, because the man is holding his glass in his left hand. Of course, the man he was painting could have been left-handed. However, people believe Vermeer was actually holding the glass in his right hand, and the mirror reversed the image. But then what hand did he paint with?

The *Procuress* is Vermeer's earliest known painting. With special X-rays, we can tell he changed his mind a few times while painting it. The men had much smaller hats at first, and the coat draped over the rug was painted in afterward. He used a **compass** to help draw the jug. With X-rays you can see a little pin prick on the **canvas** where the point went in!

The Astronomer

Around 1668, a man in his late thirties posed for Vermeer for two similar pictures with a science theme. Called *The Astronomer* and *The Geographer*, they were probably painted for the same customer. Both the **astronomer** and **geographer** are dressed in gowns, traditional for this sort of portrait.

The book lying in front of the astronomer is so detailed it can be identified! It is the 1621 edition of a book by Adriaen Metius, called *On the Investigation or Observation of the Stars*.

Two Mysteries on the Wall

On the wall is a painting of *The Finding of Moses*, which also appears in another of Vermeer's paintings. Did Vermeer paint it? It would be one more picture by Vermeer to add to the list of his missing works. No one is too sure what that curious diagram on the cupboard means, either.

The Astronomer, **1668.** The model in this picture and *The Geographer* look like the same man, possibly Antony van Leeuwenhoek, a scientist friend of Vermeer's, and inventor of a powerful **microscope**.

The Geographer

The *Astronomer* and *The Geographer* were Vermeer's only two known paintings of a lone man. Most of his paintings were of women. We are not sure who bought the two paintings, but we know they were sold by an **anonymous** owner in 1713 for "a considerable sum" of 300 florins.

Maps

The globes in the paintings were made by Jodocus Hondius in 1600, and popular at the time. One globe showed the skies, the other, the Earth, Maps were often in Vermeer's paintings, and important in Dutch life. Maps were displayed for practical reasons, for prestige, or simply as wall decorations. The globe in *The Geographer* is turned to show the Indian Ocean. This route was taken by the Dutch traders to reach China and Japan. In this painting the globe is a symbol of Dutch exploration and power.

The Geographer, 1669. Although there are differences in details between the rooms in *The Astronomer* and *The Geographer*, the room seems to be the same one, with the same corner cupboard, carpet, globes, table, and window.

Girl with a Pearl Earring

Probably the most well-known of Vermeer's paintings, *Girl with a Pearl Earring*, is recognized as Vermeer's greatest achievement. Little is known about the girl. In the Netherlands it was common to paint "tronies," which were heads, rather than portraits. The person who sat for the painting was not important, as it wasn't a portrait as such, but a study of an expression or a character.

Bargain Buy

Arnoldus Andries des Tombe bought Vermeer's *Girl with a Pearl Earring* in 1881 at a sale in The Hague for two guilders plus the auction house's 30 cent fee—a bargain for a priceless Vermeer! Only after the picture was cleaned and the signature was clear did he know it was by Vermeer.

The way that the girl looks over her shoulder makes you think you are the one who has made the girl turn her head. Do you like this painting?

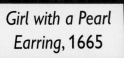

Girl with a Pearl
Earring, 1665

Vermeer's Colors

Paint wasn't sold in handy jars and tubes like it is today. There were only a few paint colors available to Vermeer. The artist would buy paint in powder form, then grind and mix the **pigment** up with water each day. Some pigments had to be used separately, as they would react with the other paint. Each color would have different drying times, thickness, and a different length of time that the color would last.

To paint blue tones, like in this painting, *The Milkmaid*, Vermeer used ultramarine. The color was made from crushed lapis lazuli, a semiprecious gem stone, and was very expensive. You could tell Vermeer was selling paintings when he could afford to paint in blue! Other painters used the cheaper pigment, azurite.

The background of *Girl with a Pearl Earring* on page 17 does not appear as it did when it came off Vermeer's easel all those years ago. Recent tests have shown that Vermeer had painted a **glaze** of green paint over the dark underpainting. The background would have been a glossy, deep green. The two pigments of the green glaze, a blue from the indigo plant and a yellow from the yellow flowers of weld, have faded over many hundred years. Paint mixing was a difficult thing!

A typical Vermeer palette would look something like this.

ultramarine

red madder

raw umber

ivory black

yellow ochre

vermilion

green earth

white lead

Who Were the Models?

In the recent film *Girl With A Pearl Earring*, the girl in the painting was said to be Vermeer's maid. No one knows who the models were, but it is more likely that some of the paintings are Vermeer's wife, Catherine. There are a series of paintings of a woman, wearing the same yellow, fur-bordered jacket. Is it the same woman? Or is it just the same jacket?

Is This Catherine?

It has been said that the woman in this and some other of Vermeer's paintings looks as if she is expecting a baby. As Catherine had 14 children it would seem quite likely that it could be her. It was very unfashionable at that time to paint pregnant women, though. Her earring looks a bit familiar, doesn't it?

Young Woman with a Pearl Necklace, painted between 1662 and 1665

The Art of Painting

Thought to be of Vermeer, this painting on the right was certainly treasured by him and his family. Vermeer did not part with it in his lifetime, even when he was very poor. After Vermeer died, his wife Catherine gave it to her mother, Maria Thins, to try and avoid having to sell it to pay off his debts. Sadly it had to be sold. After some years, with no signature, people thought the painting was by another artist, whose signature was even forged onto the painting. Then, a Vermeer scholar recognized it as a Vermeer original, and it was put in a museum in Austria.

A Prisoner of War!

During World War II, the Nazis invaded Austria. *The Art of Painting* was bought by Adolf Hitler for his personal collection. At the end of the war, the painting was rescued from a salt mine where it had been hidden from the bombing raids. *The Art of Painting* was escorted back to Austria by Andrew Ritchie, who locked himself and the painting in a train compartment to keep it safe!

The Art of Painting

Camera Obscura

Many people think Vermeer used a **camera obscura** to help him paint. His camera obscura would have used a small hole to focus light from a scene onto the back wall of Vermeer's room. The image would be upside-down, but using mirrors it is possible to project a right-side-up image. You can then trace the image onto canvas.

The Evidence

Many of Vermeer's paintings take place in the same room. By figuring out where Vermeer could have placed his camera obscura, experts have found that the image that would have been projected on the wall is exactly the same size as the various paintings that Vermeer did. Is that just a coincidence?

The Glass of Wine, painted around 1660. The large chair in the foreground may mean this image was traced using a camera obscura. Artists of the time would have painted the chair smaller, but a camera obscura would have shown the chair as large, like this.

Paint a Vermeer

Why not try and make a **collage** of your own Vermeer? Put your subject in the left-hand corner of a room. Vermeer almost always did. Why? The side wall had a window to light the scene and the far wall acted as a background. A right-handed artist usually paints with the light coming from the left so that the shadow made by his hand doesn't go over the canvas where he is painting.

Choose an almost square piece of paper for your collage. Vermeer's canvases were often this shape. Leave the painting unsigned. Vermeer only signed three of his paintings!

Woman Holding a Balance,
painted around 1664

What You'll Need

To make your collage look like a proper Vermeer, try finding pictures like these in magazines. Cut them out and make your collage. Have fun!

You could even paint a cardboard frame for your finished collage.

Vermeer's Legacy

Vermeer was 43 when he died. His wife Catherine said he died as a result of the great burden of his children, and having no money. She said he "in a day or day and a half had gone from being healthy to being dead." Vermeer was a caring father who struggled to earn enough to feed his large family. He fell into a deep depression and never recovered.

Dead and Forgotten

Vermeer was buried at the Old Church in Delft. After his death Vermeer was forgotten by the art world for more than 200 years. His few pictures were thought to be by other artists. Only in 1866, when the French critic Théophile Thoré-Bürger "rediscovered" him, did Vermeer's works become widely known.

The Old Church in Delft

MISSING!

In 1696 an auction catalog of paintings collected by Vermeer's friend Pieter van Ruijven listed paintings that have never been found. One picture is described as a portrait of Vermeer. It could be *The Art of Painting*, still in Vermeer's possession at the time of his death, but the painting only sold for 40 guilders, too low for such a large, important work of art. Perhaps this was a lost portrait of Vermeer?

Another painting, of a man washing his hands, has also never been found. Also, there are two paintings described as "a view of a house in Delft" and "a view of some houses by Vermeer." Since only Vermeer's *Little Street* fits either description, one of the paintings is now lost. Maybe one day it will be found!

Glossary

anonymous
(uh-NAH-nuh-mus)
Made or done by
someone unknown.

astronomer
(uh-STRAH-nuh-mer)
A scientist who studies
matter in outer space.

camera obscura
(KAM-ruh ub-SKYUR-uh)
A darkened chamber in
which an image of an
object is projected through
a small opening or lens.

canvas (KAN-ves)
A piece of cloth used as
a surface for painting.

Catholic (KATH-lik)
A Christian whose leader
is the pope.

collage (kuh-LAHJ)
Art made by gluing
different materials to a
flat surface.

compass (KUM-pus)
An instrument for
drawing circles.

geographer
(jee-AH-gruh-fer)
A scientist who studies
the earth.

glaze (GLAYZ)
Color that is thinned
and brushed over a
painted area to change
the original color.

microscope
(MY-kruh-skohp)
An instrument which
makes magnified images
of tiny objects using lenses.

pigment (PIG-ment)
A powder mixed with a
liquid to give color.

porcelain (POR-suh-lin)
A hard white ceramic used
to make dishes and tiles.

Protestant
(PRAH-tes-tunt)
A member of a Christian
church that separated
from the Roman Catholic
church in the 16th century.

Websites

For web resources related to the
subject of this book, go to:
www.windmillbooks.com/weblinks
and select this book's title.

Read More

Mis, Melody S. *Vermeer. Meet the Artist.* New York: PowerKids Press, 2008.

Raczka, Bob. *The Vermeer Interviews: Conversations with Seven Works of Art.* Minneapolis, MN: First Avenue Editions, 2010.

Venezia, Mike. *Johannes Vermeer.* Getting to Know the World's Greatest Artists. Danbury, CT: Children's Press, 2003.

Index